Stirrings

Oguchi H. Nkwocha

ARPress

ARPress
45 Dan Road Suite 5
Canton MA 02021
Hotline: 1(888) 821-0229
Fax: 1(508) 545-7580

Ordering Information:
Quantity sales. Special discounts are available on quantity purchases by corporations, associations, and others. For details, contact the publisher at the address above.

Printed in the United States of America.

ISBN-13:   Softcover   979-8-89676-062-7
                  eBook   979-8-89676-064-1
                  Hardback   979-8-89676-063-4

Library of Congress Control Number: 2025901209

Table of Contents

To Gail: She pointed the way at last

ℱOREWORD

Dear friend,

There is a reason for your coming in contact with this tiny volume. As you well know, size does not equate with value.

All is not well by appearance—just look around you—no matter what your doctrinal, dogmatic, or ideological persuasion. Ask yourself if you are indeed happy.

Yet all is well, in truth, and right here and now! That is how it was originally meant to be, and that is how it must be, now and forever.

Time may arc into aeons, and space stretch into infinity, if that is what it must take for you to realize your destiny. For you must become the truth that you are and nothing else.

STIRRINGS

How long can you sleep
Sedated by ineffectual doctrines and dogma
Mesmerized in an illusory dream
Shackled by webs of customary savvy
Enslaved by false beliefs
Educated in ignorant principles
Humiliated by disease and famine?
How long can we sleep
Hiding in time and space to avoid eternity
Courting death to escape immortality
Fabricating vivid illusions to eschew reality
Dividing and separating to spurn unity
Inventing guilt and conflict to spite serenity
Invoking sin and punishment to undo love?
Sleep no more; dream no more
Rise, know yourself, be yourself
For thus you find the truth of what you are
Made in all aspects like your Maker
One with Him and all creation
At once complete, perfect in all ways
Outside of which nothing exists.

HOME

I ask not for freedom of thought
But freedom from thought;
I ask not for freedom of speech
But freedom from speech
Nor freedom to act
Rather than freedom from action.
For slavery now is cloaked
In such "freedoms."
Yet beyond the mundane engagements
Of thoughts and speech and actions
Yes, of so-called freedoms,
There remains *the center.*
A domain of pure thought,
Of sheer action
And pristine freedom.
Here is my desire.

Union

But that there be no illusions
No two bodies can ever be joined
Try as you may.
And that there be no mistakes
No two minds ever can be separate
Though we try.
Such is our conviction:
The realization that all mind is one
The knowledge that two bodies
In the service of the same mind
In conjunction must be.
So may we affirm:
"What God has joined is one;
Is indeed whole forever."

NOSTALGIA

Remember, oh my soul, remember
When there was no counting
No numbers because nothing was
Beyond one, or unity?
Do you recall, my soul,
Do you recall,
When there were no words,
No language because nothing
Need be said but was at once
Known and understood?
Who invented time, clock?
Of whom is the contradiction, change?
How could you forget, my soul,
How can you, about
Love, purity, holiness,
Freedom, peace, sharing?
And for what?
But you know that the false romance
With space and time, such illusion,
Must lead us back to our wont.

A PLEA

Dear self,
Consider your relationship with me:
Love-hate, ambivalent, unrealistic.
First you ennoble me to deity,
And therefore expect immortality of me.
But you have preprogrammed me
For destruct and death.
You garnish me with ornaments,
Clothe me with all manner of comfort,
While alive; and even at death,
Lavish me with more exotic material.
Yet my lot consists in dust and decay,
Food for worms, feast for microbes.
You have projected your essence on me,
Therefore am I supposed to be almighty.
But you sabotage me with doubt
And limitations galore, and hence
Recompense me with disease and pain
For lack of fealty, and malfeasance.
I am the medium of your dreams
Of peace, love and comfort;
Yet the instrument of your attack,

Hatred, and nefariousness;
The sole basis of your preferences
And only criterion for your prejudices.
From cradle you expend
All your resources on me
Yet surely anticipating my demise.
Dear self,
May I venture to make a suggestion?
I am really only an instrument,
Devoted entirely to your service.
I am not you; could not take your place.
But I can and will perform perfectly,
Whatever task you perfectly command.
I will remain ageless, immortal,
And spotless, as you wish.
Gold and fur and perfumes I do not need;
But this I ask of you:
Thy will be done!
For only in this
Is my consummation.
Sincerely,
Your Body.

DESTINY OF MAN

To think natural
Is to think with God
To will truly
Is to share God's will
To live
Is to be of God.
For there is nought
Outside of God.
There is only one law,
The law of God,
One love, the love of God.
To see clearly
Is to have God-vision.
To speak rightly
Is to echo God's words.
And the thought of God,
Life, will, law, love,
Vision, voice: yes,
Is all one—God.
To know this
Is to be free;

To live as such
Is salvation
And finally the destiny
Of all humanity.

ILLUSION

Complexity marks illusion
Just as simplicity
Is the nature of truth.
Hence beware the if's and but's,
The exceptions and exemptions
Of worldly knowledge.
Illusions and lies—
They always build a cascade
On imaginary foundations
Adorned with alluring camouflage.
Even now,
See how it ruptures here,
Then there;
See how it leaks there,
Despite a thousand patches here.
Yet is this bulbous nothing
Imbued with the power of reality.
Truth, in the meantime
Remains calm and not threatened
Never needing defense,
Not prone to seek justification.
There is not a question though

About the outcome
But that the sheer purity
Of simplicity, truth,
Must prevail at all times.

Ego

Born in sacrifice and agony
Compelled through the rituals
Of collective evolution
Is the son of man.
Lifespan predetermined
Constrained within a life-style
Of ecological economy
Such is the son of man.
As a child, afraid of the dark
In maturity, frightened by the illumination
Of discerning light
That is the son of man
Always transactions in illusory symbols
Yet an occasional glimpse in dreams
Of another reality
This is the son of man.
Happy and sad, love and hate
Rife with the inconsistencies
Of constant conflict
The Ego is the son of man.

SELF

Created by extension of Thought
Integral part of the Source
All attributes imbued without exception
Such is the nature of Self.
Same as the Christ
Omniscient, omnipotent, glorious
Unity without fragmentation
That is the Self.
Knowing obviating understanding
Never changing, always love
Being without existing
This is the Self.
Creator and Thought and Self
All is but one,
Yes, perfectly one, without division
God is the Self.

PEACE

To be sure, peace is our heritage
A basic characteristic
Formulated by the same mechanism
As our creation.
Do we know who we are?
If so, then we know peace
And we are peace.
Yet have we no knowledge
Of what we are.
Hence are we compelled
To recite the age-old plea
"PEACE IN OUR TIME"
It is a prayer without an answer,
For a wrong question
Never will yield the correct answer.
It did not work then,
Neither will it now.
Amidst the din of our search
So well-meaning, well-intended
For peace,
Would that we remain still

For a moment in time
To look within, to find the real Self
And in so doing, will *for all times*
Peace on earth.

PROMISE

Be gentle with me today
For I still am not where I ought to be.
My sight is yet clouded
With the trappings of usual living.
My mind, the part that wanders,
Has yet to disengage from routine ruminations.
I still languish in the same illusions
Replete with conflict and insecurities.
All around me are symbols
Seemingly solidified in reality.
Therefore have I despaired,
A weakling unable to seriously impact my lot.
For the symbols, oh how they scream
Of lack and disease and death,
Miserly begrudging a laughter here,
And a little fun there,
All the while laced with fear
Even as the inevitable clock ticks.
Be certain of one thing though:
I know my place;
I know correct vision.
My mind has never left its source—

It cannot!

Nor has it forgotten my purpose.

Even now I begin the journey

That fulfills my purpose

And I live to laugh at the folly

Of symbolism

And the flimsy nature of illusions.

I join the light of my real Self;

Light that casts no shadows

And knows no flux,

Effortlessly dismissing death and rot;

Light that does not mark time,

But reveals timelessness.

Of this, be sure.

VISION

The sighted are leading the blind
Where sight is not vision
So indeed do the blind lead the blind.
Sight is the scotoma
Fashioned by the eyes
Interpreted by a perjured brain
Misdirected by a confused mind
Accepted by unchallenged false belief.
Hence it indeed is so—
Believing is seeing.
Enter vision
An act of extension,
Of sharing;
An experience of communion in light,
Always the one field—
Love, peace, joy and happiness;
Oneness and wholeness.
Vision is thought,
The original thought;
It is mind,
The original mind.

One man with vision
Can save the whole humanity;
A thousand men with perfect sight
Could not even guide a babe.

QUEST

Hidden in the restlessness of youth
Is an unnamed search,
A gnawing want of something
Beyond immediate reach.
In the apparent calmness of senescence
Conceals a tumultuous longing
For demise to unlock the puzzle,
Life having failed to yield an answer.
A little while longer
The infant loses its innocence
Looking both deprived and disappointed,
Compelled to join the ranks of unfulfilled humanity.
Meanwhile the search continues in utter darkness
Occasionally faintly illuminated
By a passing distant star.
Confused, confounded and bruised
Man weaves a system of illusion
Which he toys with and dubs reality
Which creates more questions than answers.
His creations haunt him;
Oh how they taunt him too,
Relentlessly hunting him down,

A victim of his own illusions.
Yet beyond his self-imposed horizon
Remains the prize;
No, it is indeed within him,
A place where he failed to look.
Here resides what he thought he lost
What he searched for in the heavens,
And dug for in the depths of the earth
Tried to substitute illusion for.
Awake then, seeker,
Be fulfilled and end your quest;
Light is here, your real Self,
God.

RELIGION

The religions of man teach sacrifice
But sacrifice is not of God.
Sacrifice implicates loss
And who can counsel
That God has lost something
Or would demand loss of His beloved?
The religions of man teach martyrdom
Yet martyrdom expresses weakness,
And silhouettes hostility and fear
Masked in false strength and indignation;
Neither is of God.
The religions of man teach exclusion
And division and ostracism,
The very hallmarks of separation
Therefore do they number in the thousands;
But God is One, one with all His creation.
Beware then,
Of the accommodation of dualities
In any doctrines.
For how can a loving God punish?
Will a living God create a dying species?
What place do aberrations have

In the expression of a perfect Source?
Would you attribute a superego to God
To turn around to worship it and kowtow
To ward off his divine-scale anger?
In vain will their priests hurry
To administer last rites—
Indeed do the dead bury the dead,
Obviously no credit to a living God
For how long will the doctrine
Of sin and guilt and hell reign?
Yet the Truth be known:
God made man in His likeness;
Nothing more need be said!

ƤURPOSE

Life but holds one purpose
So simple but natural and powerful
Yet often not realized
As we enrapture in ostentatious plans.
Such plans as lead in various courses
Always divergent, always competitive
In the end obscuring apparently
The original purpose.
As for the courses,
They become endless circular motion,
With nebulous and shifting activity,
Without a viable center, aimless.
Thus we plod along at various speeds,
Some in haste and impatience,
Some with lazy leisure;
Always the unvoiced question—whither?
Yes, where can purpose be found,
And what is it?
Surely not high living nor high learning
Not in pleasure or deprivation.
Valor and cowardice,
Sacrifice and avarice,

Wisdom and blissful ignorance,

All alike fall short of purpose.

But to look at another

And see perfection and love,

An exact reflection of you,

To know and treat them thusly;

To realise your oneness

With all creation and the Creator,

Yes, to be alive, and love, as one

Never again knowing separation;

Forever dispensing with strife and conflict,

Dissolving finally the illusion

Of time and space,

To bask in eternal harmony now—

That is purpose.

GUIDE

You are ready to journey
To your true home
Of which you constantly dream,
For the dreamer must awaken.
Your guide is ready—
Always has been.
He will navigate you
Through territory uncharted
But have no fear,
For he too has been there.
A constant companion,
A patient comrade,
A reference source and consultant
At all times.
In your fulfillment is He fulfilled,
For you are one, united with Him.
Linger no longer then;
Gird your loins and be off.
How long will you tarry?
What longer does it hold for you
This place of no consequence,
A place that is no place at all?

At the best of times
You glimpsed even better,
Though mostly it was a struggle.
Now your whole being restlessly stirs;
Like must return to like,
Spirit to spirit, mind to mind.
Yet is there no distance to cover,
For you are already
Where you ready yourself to go
Could the Creator really leave Himself?
Neither could the Son of God.

GUIDANCE

Be glad, my soul, for I am guided;
My mind is formatted
For the only goal for which I am here.
My course is so charted
That all routes lead to the only goal
For which I was created.
Within me is an indelible template
Of light and love
Of my true identity,
Lest I should forget.
And how can I forget,
Though I am enmeshed in earthly events?
I am only reminded at each turn,
With every earthly transaction,
That I am an alien here:
Therefore do I even yearn more
For what I really am.
And an alien indeed;
What part, I ask, have I
In the illusion that is the world
But to stamp a mark of reality on it?
Even though I may appear

To flounder in time
As I confront merely evanescent darkness,
Let there be no doubt nor question
But that I am guided.
I am branded with serenity,
With love and joy and power,
With wholeness and everlasting happiness.
I bear the peaceful mark
Of my Creator at all times
As do my brothers, every last one.
And we all are one.
That is guidance.

Null

There is no truth in duality;

If it is not One, then it is nought.

If it dies, it was never alive,

Because there is no death in life.

Darkness and light could not coexist,

Nor could light cast a shadow.

If it changes and fluctuates,

Then it is not real.

Reality is absolute,

Without grade or shade.

Love feels only love;

Nothing else can it experience.

If it has a boundary,

Then it is divided; it is not one;

It cannot be of God.

Judgement is discriminatory

Therefore separates;

God has no act of judgement.

Nor has He any use for it.

Hence trust not your perception

If it would present duality

For that is not of your real self.

Place not your trust in numbers
Which formalize your belief
In separation and illusion;
For there is only One.
Should the concepts of duality
At anytime be a stumbling block,
When you are tempted by any other
Than truth and reality,
Dismiss them with confidence,
For they are null;
Only God is.

PROGRESS

Your direction is assured.
Love attracts you to itself.
Go on; the prize is waiting.
No longer vacillate,
No more uncertain pauses;
Light beckons you
With steady luminance.
Even now all takes on a new look
All is changing.
Peace awaits you,
Joy is your prize.
Oneness welcomes you
For there is but One.
Maybe an occasional glance back
Maybe temporary backsliding
Not to worry; your course is sure.
Happiness is your birthright,
Could not be fulfilled without you
It calls out your name.
Because that too is its name
All your brothers await you,
And there you will discover

To your delight
That you, they, we—
All are One, is one indeed.
Bid farewell to dreams:
Who needs dreams
In the domain of reality?
Reality is truth
What else could exist
Outside of truth?
Advance then to reality,
To truth, your real self;
Come home to God.

ℒIFE

Joy is the basis of life

Joy is everlasting

As life is eternal

Joy manifests life;

To experience one

Is to know the other.

Happiness is the fabric of life

It is constant

Just as life is forever

Happiness suffuses life;

One could not be

Without the other.

Love is life

Love never fades

As life never dies

Love substantiates life;

Where one exists

Must be the other.

Peace is the context of life

Peace is unending

Just as life is endless

Peace sustains life;

To have one
Is to have the other
Oneness is the secret of life
It is whole
As life is one
Oneness characterizes life;
To experience one
Is to live the other.

SHADOWS

Our constant preoccupation
With the pursuit of happiness
Is the attestation
To its reality;
Yet we know not how
Or what its substance is.
We seek love
With all manner of involvement
For our instincts reassure us
That it must be real;
But we have not experienced
Nor known its form.
We desire to prolong life
At the cost of all,
In so doing
Hinting at eternity;
Yet do we not know the privilege
Or the essence of it.
Tradition locks us into molds
Whereby we only dream
Of the shadows of reality
Banished by our own customs

To the outermost periphery
Of what is possible;
Forever condemned
To compete with one another
For the mere pittance
That defines the extent
Of our concept and perception.
The time must come
When at last we realize
That the subject of our dreams,
The object of our desires,
The goal of all our search
And the prize of our efforts
Is the only reality of what we are;
What we already are.
Finally we will live what we are.

REASON

Come now and let us reason together:
What have you benefited
From all the years of carrying on
As if you were a mere body?
Maybe your life span has been eked out some,
But what awaits you with nefarious relish?
Day and night you slave away on the one hand
So you can feed and clothe and romance a body;
On the other hand you despise and spite it
Because it certainly will fail you in due course.
You have faithfully followed an ancient tradition
Of blind worship of mere organic matter,
Dutifully falling in line to attempt the impossible—
The deification of the flesh.
Just think: What if you are not a body?
Great possibilities open up
Even for the body too.

NOTICE

Be it known that my ways are changed
From wonted habits and customs
From worldly wisdom and counsel
From accepted dogma and doctrine.
For these modi operandi
Have assured failure and inadequacy
And supported lack and war,
Guilt and separation and disease.
Worldly wisdom impresses me not
See for yourself; consider the outcome,
From global danger to personal insecurity.
The best of us are quartered the same way
By insidious and tiny microbes
Just as the lowliest mendicant;
Save for an occasional saviour
Whose message is soon forgotten
Mostly wasted on a population
Self-compelled to hide from light
And revel in guilt and hurt.
Though indeed many see the problem
And seek various solutions

Yet is there but one solution
Because there is only one problem
Despite protean manifestations.
So have many turned to religion
Only to be disillusioned
With the constant call for sacrifice
And continuous harangue over sin and hell
Offering a tiny Band-Aid for a gaping wound,
Eager to give last rites in the place of life
Teaching love and prayer and worship
To a god who must be enhanced and appeased
By men bruising their knees, in competition,
Begging and pleading for divine mercies
And for supplies from a limited stock.
Little wonder nothing's changed for the better;
This god has no more to offer
Than a mere mortal:
Not then nor now, neither in the future.
Today I seek my true identity
Which no illusion can obscure,
No tradition corrupt;
Nor can time tarnish.
Created as love light and purity

For joy and peace and happiness
With singular perfection:
All my brothers and I, together as one
By life itself in the eternal now
The One and Oneness—God.

HOMEWARD

As the compass sets to the true north
So is my path pointed homeward
For I have no other destiny.
Though the storms of earthly living
Stir up dark clouds and dense fog
I maintain an even keel to a certain destination.
The waves may crash and bash the craft
And possibilities for running aground abound
Yet assured is arrival at homeport.
A few tempting islands scattered in the sea of life
Plenty of other promising alternative landing sites
But none like it, no substitute for real home.
Easily I may fall prey to worldly sleep and dreams
Be victimized by popular sense and worldly science
Yet my navigator is faithful, on autopilot.
Like the welcoming crowd awaits the docking
So my family awaits my return with joy and celebration
For I am loved; have been gone too long.
As with a returning traveller—a sweet surprise at home:
All is well; the family is intact, one;
For there was never even a separation.
And yet even before I get there

I sense I am not a lone boat on a unique trip:
We all are making the same journey; direction, same.
I now know that there is no separate entity
From the One, nor from one another,
Any more than a drop can claim individuality from the sea.
And also that there is no distance to cover
Despite illusions, and seeming appearances
For home has always been with us, even at this moment.

ᛈRAYER

When prayer turns into begging
It becomes a ploy to influence policy
Surely one does not expect God to participate.
When prayer calls for fasting
An exercise in self-flagellation and purification
How could God have anything to do with it?
When prayer demands justification
When prayer is a supplication
Certainly God is not addressed.
If prayer asks for prior- or post-appreciation
If prayer asks for forgiveness
God is not part of it.
Yet are you taught to ask for victory over another
Or to pray for your enemies
Terms that mean nothing to God.
If you desire to ask correctly
You must look to the workings of your mind
Here you accept something and it becomes yours.
Yet part of your mind is deceived with illusions
And alas, this is your usual station.
But your real mind ever abides in you.
The lessons of your real mind are thus:

You have no separate existence from God,
Nor from one another though you call him enemy.
Your mind is part of, and one with the mind of God
All that God has is therefore yours as it is one
And all you have to do is accept what is already yours
God knows no needs, neither should you.
If it is God, then it is abundant
It is also for all and all are truly one
You need not attempt to qualify for eligibility
You need not purify yourself beforehand
For God knows you as pure and perfect, being His handiwork
Ideally, and most certainly in due course,
There is no place for prayer;
But while we must pray, let it be
An act of remembrance and identification,
An acceptance of who and what we already are.

$SHAM

At the basis of anger
Is a sense of frustration
A hint of helplessness
A feeling of loss of worth
A suggestion of vulnerability
And the perception of hurt
Therefore evoking a reaction
Of rage and outrage,
Hostility and attack,
Revenge and punishment
A display of brutality
And indignation.
Such is the force of anger
It seems to possess
Like an alien power
Completely blinding
Bypassing reason and judgement.
Yet there is no justification
And no reason for anger
Where there is knowledge
Of the source of anger.
For anger is a quality of the ego

That thrives on separatist scheme
And paranoid ideation.
But more important is the fact
Of oneness with all creation,
Therefore of agreement with all;
The realization of unity with God
Therefore of love and power limitless
The knowledge of the perfect nature of all
Hence proving faultlessness.
Anger and the reason for it
Are woven in illusions,
As such, baseless, nonexistent
And without an ounce of justification.
The best defense against anger
Is always the recalling of truth.

Shadow

Come with me to the mountaintop:
Behold the panorama
The beauty that is the landscape
Of your earthly dwelling place
See here the silver gleam of the noon sun
As the gentle stream quietly threads it seaward.
And there the flora compose a song of colors
Where the fauna revel in the music.
Better still take the vantage point
Of the cold airless space
And contrast the exquisite blue planet
Warm with beauty, inviting as nostalgia
Spinning its dance to unknown rhythms
Carefully brooding, with maternal concern,
The life and times of humanity.
Open your eyes and look again
For this is nothing
A mere shadow of shadows
An imperfect projection of incomplete pictures
No reality here, my friend,
No intrinsic beauty or native rhythm
Only the content of part of your mind

That part confused with separation
A no-thing that never happened
Though believed, taught and expounded
If what you see you think is beautiful
Then wait until you have vision
Until you know love and experience life.
Now come down from that mountain,
From outer space.
Close your eyes,
Meet your real Self
Be Oneness.

ENIGMA

It becomes unimaginable
How anything but perfect
Could hatch out of perfection
Could time and space make a loop
Issuing out of eternity
To pinch it off into tiny segments?
Whenever did life beget death
Or death embellish the cycle of life?
Who can separate what is forever whole
What will subdivide absolute oneness?
Where has one established mind autonomous
Or created self independent?
There is no station for change
In the field of timelessness,
Of eternal now.
Relax, there is no conflict
Or comparison of opposites
The illusion that made the enigma
Is but a nebulous ephemeral bluff
Making no impact, leaving no blemish.
Son of God, you are One with your Maker.

REPLY

Dear Body,

Until now you were misunderstood,

Mistaken, misused, mortified and crucified.

I have heard your plea

And I know your problem;

Now I have the answer.

Henceforth will you not be used

As an instrument of attack

As a symbol of separation or uniqueness

For truly neither are you.

Your function is to serve

As medium of communication

In a system which believes in such media.

You are the servant rather than the served

Yours is to perfectly respond

To the direction of the mind

Which bears total responsibility

For cause and effect.

In this you must rejoice

Seeing that the mind now knows its place

For no longer will it seek to recapture

What it falsely thought it had lost

By deifying, and immortalizing you,
A futile act at best.
Now the mind knows
That like belongs with like
Mind with Mind
Separation being impossible
As all there ever is
Is one, wholesome Oneness.
When you are employed
By the Mind for the Mind
Divinity has suffused you
Perfection recreates you
Life and love animate you
And ah, heavenly fulfillment.
Anything else you must ignore
For it could not apply to you
There being only one reality
One truth, one Love, one Light
And now you are in it.
With the same Love, from
The Self.

SHIRK

How easy it is to continue
To attempt the impossible
Thereby avoiding the possible
Hoping as such to ignore the obvious.
For how else to describe humanity
Which constantly seeks out darkness
Rather than embrace light;
Busily weaving complicated life-webs
So to scorn elegant simplicity.
He aims to construct a separate reality
That he may deny his true identity.
He would undertake to move mountains
One grain of sand and rock at a time
When he could just say a word
And disperse the entire universe.
He concocts a system of illusions
Enmeshing himself thoroughly in it
Then tries to imbue it with reality
All the while rejecting the only reality.
He excels in the subject of love
Wherein is invested hatred and guilt
Augmented by punishment and jealousy

Therefore spiting the purity of love.
He often lingers in the past
Or lounges in the future;
Time is entirely his invention
But timelessness, now, is his real home.
To attempt to run away from oneself
Is but to shirk one's responsibilities
Wasting energy at the impossible
While the possible waits in easy reach.

ROOT

No matter what your pleasure
In difficulties or neuroses
Whatever your fixation
Or incurable disease
Maybe it is a brand
Of lack or fear or insecurity
Perhaps it is clothed
In flowing and insurmountable odds
Leaving you parched and hungry
Is it anger or hatred
Guilt and envy and competition
Hurt or loss or anguish
Frustration and sacrifice and avarice?
Pare down any problem to the core
Recognize a theme of commonality
Dissect any puzzle to the bare bones
Find the same elemental basic
For there cannot be more than singular
Like a tree with various appendages
Yet supported by only one root
Separation is the culprit
Belief in its reality earns conflict

Conflict has protean manifestations

Yet separation is a false concept

So has no basis and no effects permanent

Truth is the answer

Truth means oneness and unity

Of one and all with their Creator

Who can separate from Oneness?

What can impact Wholeness?

Oneness is love and peace

Joy and life and happiness

If you see a problem

The answer is already there

In reality

There is no problem

CREDO

Only two options, one choice
In all of life's transactions
But in reality only one
For the other is nought.

Forms and grades and numbers
Let them not scare you
Though they movingly impress you
For they have no substance.

The ghost is as solid
As the belief that sustains it
For the void can only be animated
By the mind that upholds it.

A feedback to its designer
Resident within its source
Such is your world
Sole fabrication of your mind.

Renegade, so thinks your mind
Separation is its premise
How delusional, how false
The product is a paranoid world.

No mind exists outside the Mind
No creation is but by the One
There is no world
If it is not by Him made.

Hence is there just one choice
One option, one way
One creation, one Being
All is One.

Dismantle illusions, disarm your world
Withdraw the allegiance to nothingness
Identify with your heritage
There is no other.

COUNSEL

Placate the din and tumult
That constitute daily living
Abandon the roar and boisterousness
Characterising usual earthly existence
Jump ship off this train of disaster
Symbol of preprogrammed tradition
Why feed thoughtlessness
To nonexistent mindlessness
And attempt to justify it
By investing it with belief?
Be still then
Amidst the thunder and crackle
Be calm
In the face of excitement
Listen
To the voice of the Self
Rest
In the Mind of the Maker
Live
As the nature of the Creator
Then discover the real world
And wonder how it was ever entertained—

The illusion in time and space
Of which neither ever existed
Know your identity
Be who you are

RESOLVE

The world that I see and experience
Is a status report
An expression of the content of my mind.
If I fail to see perfection
Then I see not at all;
Thus must my mind be deluded
To suppose that it is separate
From the one Mind
A proposition so desperate, so impossible
For the mind of God is perfection
And that is the only Mind.
It must be peace and happiness
Wholeness, oneness and timelessness
Otherwise it is not of God,
Therefore does not, cannot exist.
Illusions I refuse to patronize;
Nor blindly continue to recognize
A world fabricated, without basis
Though it be the dominant tradition.
For I am the extension of God my maker
And I must have His vision and attributes
As a matter of course and fact.

My true and only world
In the mind of God belongs and exists:
I must realize who I am
And be what I am.

FUNCTION

Mine is not to serve the ego
In obedience of powerless customs
Lacking authority other than tradition
Engrossed in conflict and pain
Nor the pursuit with illusion
Of different shades of same illusion
The domain of expertise
Of the disguising ego
Yet what substance has the ego
Being that its sustenance
Is the ever-obliging false belief
In an impossible idea—separation?
Mine is not to fuel the smoke
The screen that is the world
A nothingness that attempts to obscure
And desperately displace the truth
Oh the futility of it all!
How can illusion countenance truth
Or idle dream spar with reality?
Clear as spring water is my function
Based on a single fact:
I am Son of God

One with Him and all His creation
All my brothers are but one and the same
One Son of God
His home is in his Father
His world is heaven
His mind is love and peace
Eternity is his place
To awaken from slumber
Wherein the notion of time and space
Of separation from the Father
Has been entertained
A false idea in reality and truth
That is my function
To recall my indelible identity
And be, accordingly